MICRODOSE JOURNAL

THIS JOURNAL BELONGS TO

_____

PHONE NUMBER

_____

ADDRESS

_____

THIS JOURNAL CONTAINS

GOALS

The goals page at the front of this journal is to write down what you hope to get out of microdosing. Some people will microdose for anxiety or depression, others creativity or focus etc. Everyone is different. Use this page to write what you wish to achieve, so you can focus your minset towards reaching these goals. Goals may change over time so it is important to update these if necessary.

JOURNAL PAGES

The journal pages are for daily reflections in both your days on and off. This will help you to track the changes your microdosing has on you, and will help you to further understand how to better improve your microdosing experience. These pages are especially useful for tracking doses and the effects they have. Even the slightest change in dose can change your whole microdosing experience, and it is crucial that you find the right does for yourself. An example journal page is found on the next page.

All the information included in these pages will be useful to track, and will ultimately lead to the most successful microdosing experience.

NOTES

The last pages of this book contains room for more notes. Each note is dated and has room for a title. Use this to write and track any key findings from your experience that might not exactly fit into a daily journal / diary entry, but remain crucial to your microdosing experience. It may also include notes of preferred dosages, goals reached or periodic reflections and updates.

USING THIS JOURNAL

Describe the dose

Note major changes or patterns

Days since last dose

Reflect on your day. Did the dose help, how are you feeling, do you feel the effects of an off dose day etc.

Other things that may affect you or your mindset

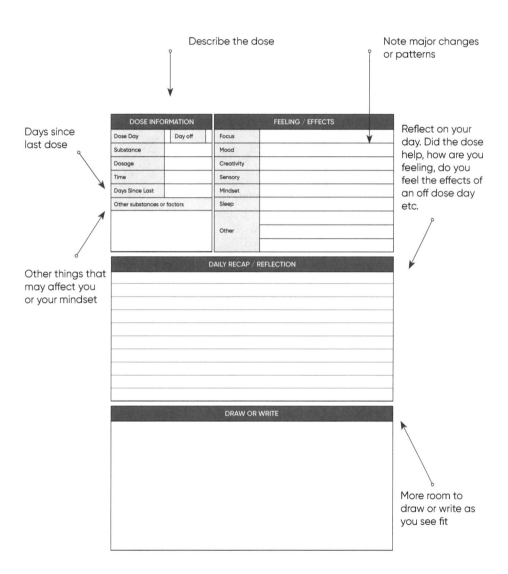

DOSE INFORMATION			FEELING / EFFECTS	
Dose Day	Day off		Focus	
Substance			Mood	
Dosage			Creativity	
Time			Sensory	
Days Since Last			Mindset	
Other substances or factors			Sleep	
			Other	

DAILY RECAP / REFLECTION

DRAW OR WRITE

More room to draw or write as you see fit

GOALS

Date	

DOSE INFORMATION

Dose Day		Day off	
Substance			
Dosage			
Time			
Days Since Last			
Other substances or factors			

FEELING / EFFECTS

Focus	
Mood	
Creativity	
Sensory	
Mindset	
Sleep	
Other	

DAILY RECAP / REFLECTION

DRAW OR WRITE

Date	

DOSE INFORMATION				FEELING / EFFECTS	
Dose Day		Day off		Focus	
Substance				Mood	
Dosage				Creativity	
Time				Sensory	
Days Since Last				Mindset	
Other substances or factors				Sleep	
				Other	

DAILY RECAP / REFLECTION

DRAW OR WRITE

Date	

DOSE INFORMATION

Dose Day		Day off	
Substance			
Dosage			
Time			
Days Since Last			
Other substances or factors			

FEELING / EFFECTS

Focus	
Mood	
Creativity	
Sensory	
Mindset	
Sleep	
Other	

DAILY RECAP / REFLECTION

DRAW OR WRITE

Date	

DOSE INFORMATION		FEELING / EFFECTS	

DOSE INFORMATION			FEELING / EFFECTS	
Dose Day	Day off		Focus	
Substance			Mood	
Dosage			Creativity	
Time			Sensory	
Days Since Last			Mindset	
Other substances or factors			Sleep	
			Other	

DAILY RECAP / REFLECTION

DRAW OR WRITE

Date	

DOSE INFORMATION			FEELING / EFFECTS	

DOSE INFORMATION			FEELING / EFFECTS	
Dose Day		Day off	Focus	
Substance			Mood	
Dosage			Creativity	
Time			Sensory	
Days Since Last			Mindset	
Other substances or factors			Sleep	
			Other	

DAILY RECAP / REFLECTION

DRAW OR WRITE

Date	

DOSE INFORMATION			
Dose Day		Day off	
Substance			
Dosage			
Time			
Days Since Last			
Other substances or factors			

FEELING / EFFECTS	
Focus	
Mood	
Creativity	
Sensory	
Mindset	
Sleep	
Other	

DAILY RECAP / REFLECTION

DRAW OR WRITE

Date	

DOSE INFORMATION

Dose Day		Day off	
Substance			
Dosage			
Time			
Days Since Last			
Other substances or factors			

FEELING / EFFECTS

Focus	
Mood	
Creativity	
Sensory	
Mindset	
Sleep	
Other	

DAILY RECAP / REFLECTION

DRAW OR WRITE

Date	

DOSE INFORMATION

Dose Day		Day off	
Substance			
Dosage			
Time			
Days Since Last			
Other substances or factors			

FEELING / EFFECTS

Focus	
Mood	
Creativity	
Sensory	
Mindset	
Sleep	
Other	

DAILY RECAP / REFLECTION

DRAW OR WRITE

Date	

DOSE INFORMATION

Dose Day		Day off	
Substance			
Dosage			
Time			
Days Since Last			
Other substances or factors			

FEELING / EFFECTS

Focus	
Mood	
Creativity	
Sensory	
Mindset	
Sleep	
Other	

DAILY RECAP / REFLECTION

DRAW OR WRITE

Date	

DOSE INFORMATION			FEELING / EFFECTS	
Dose Day	Day off		Focus	
Substance			Mood	
Dosage			Creativity	
Time			Sensory	
Days Since Last			Mindset	
Other substances or factors			Sleep	
			Other	

DAILY RECAP / REFLECTION

DRAW OR WRITE

Date	

DOSE INFORMATION

Dose Day		Day off	
Substance			
Dosage			
Time			
Days Since Last			
Other substances or factors			

FEELING / EFFECTS

Focus	
Mood	
Creativity	
Sensory	
Mindset	
Sleep	
Other	

DAILY RECAP / REFLECTION

DRAW OR WRITE

Date	

DOSE INFORMATION

Dose Day		Day off	
Substance			
Dosage			
Time			
Days Since Last			
Other substances or factors			

FEELING / EFFECTS

Focus	
Mood	
Creativity	
Sensory	
Mindset	
Sleep	
Other	

DAILY RECAP / REFLECTION

DRAW OR WRITE

Date	

DOSE INFORMATION			FEELING / EFFECTS		
Dose Day		Day off	Focus		
Substance			Mood		
Dosage			Creativity		
Time			Sensory		
Days Since Last			Mindset		
Other substances or factors			Sleep		
			Other		

DAILY RECAP / REFLECTION

DRAW OR WRITE

Date	

DOSE INFORMATION

Dose Day		Day off	
Substance			
Dosage			
Time			
Days Since Last			
Other substances or factors			

FEELING / EFFECTS

Focus	
Mood	
Creativity	
Sensory	
Mindset	
Sleep	
Other	

DAILY RECAP / REFLECTION

DRAW OR WRITE

Date	

DOSE INFORMATION

Dose Day		Day off	
Substance			
Dosage			
Time			
Days Since Last			
Other substances or factors			

FEELING / EFFECTS

Focus	
Mood	
Creativity	
Sensory	
Mindset	
Sleep	
Other	

DAILY RECAP / REFLECTION

DRAW OR WRITE

Date	

DOSE INFORMATION			FEELING / EFFECTS	
Dose Day		Day off	Focus	
Substance			Mood	
Dosage			Creativity	
Time			Sensory	
Days Since Last			Mindset	
Other substances or factors			Sleep	
			Other	

DAILY RECAP / REFLECTION

DRAW OR WRITE

Date	

DOSE INFORMATION			FEELING / EFFECTS	
Dose Day	Day off		Focus	
Substance			Mood	
Dosage			Creativity	
Time			Sensory	
Days Since Last			Mindset	
Other substances or factors			Sleep	
			Other	

DAILY RECAP / REFLECTION

DRAW OR WRITE

Date	

DOSE INFORMATION

Dose Day		Day off	
Substance			
Dosage			
Time			
Days Since Last			
Other substances or factors			

FEELING / EFFECTS

Focus	
Mood	
Creativity	
Sensory	
Mindset	
Sleep	
Other	

DAILY RECAP / REFLECTION

DRAW OR WRITE

Date	

DOSE INFORMATION				FEELING / EFFECTS	
Dose Day		Day off		Focus	
Substance				Mood	
Dosage				Creativity	
Time				Sensory	
Days Since Last				Mindset	
Other substances or factors				Sleep	
				Other	

DAILY RECAP / REFLECTION

DRAW OR WRITE

Date	

DOSE INFORMATION

Dose Day		Day off	
Substance			
Dosage			
Time			
Days Since Last			
Other substances or factors			

FEELING / EFFECTS

Focus	
Mood	
Creativity	
Sensory	
Mindset	
Sleep	
Other	

DAILY RECAP / REFLECTION

DRAW OR WRITE

Date	

DOSE INFORMATION			FEELING / EFFECTS		
Dose Day		Day off	Focus		
Substance			Mood		
Dosage			Creativity		
Time			Sensory		
Days Since Last			Mindset		
Other substances or factors			Sleep		
			Other		

DAILY RECAP / REFLECTION

DRAW OR WRITE

Date	

DOSE INFORMATION

Dose Day		Day off	
Substance			
Dosage			
Time			
Days Since Last			
Other substances or factors			

FEELING / EFFECTS

Focus	
Mood	
Creativity	
Sensory	
Mindset	
Sleep	
Other	

DAILY RECAP / REFLECTION

DRAW OR WRITE

Date	

DOSE INFORMATION

Dose Day		Day off	
Substance			
Dosage			
Time			
Days Since Last			
Other substances or factors			

FEELING / EFFECTS

Focus	
Mood	
Creativity	
Sensory	
Mindset	
Sleep	
Other	

DAILY RECAP / REFLECTION

DRAW OR WRITE

Date	

DOSE INFORMATION			FEELING / EFFECTS	
Dose Day	Day off		Focus	
Substance			Mood	
Dosage			Creativity	
Time			Sensory	
Days Since Last			Mindset	
Other substances or factors			Sleep	
			Other	

DAILY RECAP / REFLECTION

DRAW OR WRITE

Date	

DOSE INFORMATION			FEELING / EFFECTS	
Dose Day	Day off		Focus	
Substance			Mood	
Dosage			Creativity	
Time			Sensory	
Days Since Last			Mindset	
Other substances or factors			Sleep	
			Other	

DAILY RECAP / REFLECTION

DRAW OR WRITE

Date	

DOSE INFORMATION			FEELING / EFFECTS	
Dose Day	Day off		Focus	
Substance			Mood	
Dosage			Creativity	
Time			Sensory	
Days Since Last			Mindset	
Other substances or factors			Sleep	
			Other	

DAILY RECAP / REFLECTION

DRAW OR WRITE

Date	

DOSE INFORMATION	

Dose Day		Day off	
Substance			
Dosage			
Time			
Days Since Last			
Other substances or factors			

FEELING / EFFECTS	
Focus	
Mood	
Creativity	
Sensory	
Mindset	
Sleep	
Other	

DAILY RECAP / REFLECTION

DRAW OR WRITE

Date	

DOSE INFORMATION

Dose Day		Day off	
Substance			
Dosage			
Time			
Days Since Last			
Other substances or factors			

FEELING / EFFECTS

Focus	
Mood	
Creativity	
Sensory	
Mindset	
Sleep	
Other	

DAILY RECAP / REFLECTION

DRAW OR WRITE

Date	

DOSE INFORMATION

Dose Day		Day off	
Substance			
Dosage			
Time			
Days Since Last			
Other substances or factors			

FEELING / EFFECTS

Focus	
Mood	
Creativity	
Sensory	
Mindset	
Sleep	
Other	

DAILY RECAP / REFLECTION

DRAW OR WRITE

Date	

DOSE INFORMATION

Dose Day		Day off	
Substance			
Dosage			
Time			
Days Since Last			
Other substances or factors			

FEELING / EFFECTS

Focus	
Mood	
Creativity	
Sensory	
Mindset	
Sleep	
Other	

DAILY RECAP / REFLECTION

DRAW OR WRITE

Date	

DOSE INFORMATION

Dose Day		Day off	
Substance			
Dosage			
Time			
Days Since Last			
Other substances or factors			

FEELING / EFFECTS

Focus	
Mood	
Creativity	
Sensory	
Mindset	
Sleep	
Other	

DAILY RECAP / REFLECTION

DRAW OR WRITE

Date	

DOSE INFORMATION

Dose Day		Day off	
Substance			
Dosage			
Time			
Days Since Last			
Other substances or factors			

FEELING / EFFECTS

Focus	
Mood	
Creativity	
Sensory	
Mindset	
Sleep	
Other	

DAILY RECAP / REFLECTION

DRAW OR WRITE

Date	

DOSE INFORMATION		
Dose Day		Day off
Substance		
Dosage		
Time		
Days Since Last		
Other substances or factors		

FEELING / EFFECTS	
Focus	
Mood	
Creativity	
Sensory	
Mindset	
Sleep	
Other	

DAILY RECAP / REFLECTION

DRAW OR WRITE

Date	

DOSE INFORMATION

Dose Day		Day off	
Substance			
Dosage			
Time			
Days Since Last			
Other substances or factors			

FEELING / EFFECTS

Focus	
Mood	
Creativity	
Sensory	
Mindset	
Sleep	
Other	

DAILY RECAP / REFLECTION

DRAW OR WRITE

Date	

DOSE INFORMATION		
Dose Day	Day off	
Substance		
Dosage		
Time		
Days Since Last		
Other substances or factors		

FEELING / EFFECTS	
Focus	
Mood	
Creativity	
Sensory	
Mindset	
Sleep	
Other	

DAILY RECAP / REFLECTION

DRAW OR WRITE

Date	

DOSE INFORMATION			FEELING / EFFECTS	
Dose Day		Day off	Focus	
Substance			Mood	
Dosage			Creativity	
Time			Sensory	
Days Since Last			Mindset	
Other substances or factors			Sleep	
			Other	

DAILY RECAP / REFLECTION

DRAW OR WRITE

Date	

DOSE INFORMATION			FEELING / EFFECTS	
Dose Day	Day off		Focus	
Substance			Mood	
Dosage			Creativity	
Time			Sensory	
Days Since Last			Mindset	
Other substances or factors			Sleep	
			Other	

DAILY RECAP / REFLECTION

DRAW OR WRITE

Date	

DOSE INFORMATION			FEELING / EFFECTS	
Dose Day		Day off	Focus	
Substance			Mood	
Dosage			Creativity	
Time			Sensory	
Days Since Last			Mindset	
Other substances or factors			Sleep	
			Other	

DAILY RECAP / REFLECTION

DRAW OR WRITE

Date	

DOSE INFORMATION			FEELING / EFFECTS	
Dose Day		Day off	Focus	
Substance			Mood	
Dosage			Creativity	
Time			Sensory	
Days Since Last			Mindset	
Other substances or factors			Sleep	
			Other	

DAILY RECAP / REFLECTION

DRAW OR WRITE

Date	

DOSE INFORMATION

Dose Day		Day off	
Substance			
Dosage			
Time			
Days Since Last			
Other substances or factors			

FEELING / EFFECTS

Focus	
Mood	
Creativity	
Sensory	
Mindset	
Sleep	
Other	

DAILY RECAP / REFLECTION

DRAW OR WRITE

Date	

DOSE INFORMATION

Dose Day		Day off	
Substance			
Dosage			
Time			
Days Since Last			
Other substances or factors			

FEELING / EFFECTS

Focus	
Mood	
Creativity	
Sensory	
Mindset	
Sleep	
Other	

DAILY RECAP / REFLECTION

DRAW OR WRITE

Date	

DOSE INFORMATION				FEELING / EFFECTS	
Dose Day		Day off		Focus	
Substance				Mood	
Dosage				Creativity	
Time				Sensory	
Days Since Last				Mindset	
Other substances or factors				Sleep	
				Other	

DAILY RECAP / REFLECTION

DRAW OR WRITE

Date	

DOSE INFORMATION			FEELING / EFFECTS	
Dose Day	Day off	Focus	
Substance		Mood	
Dosage		Creativity	
Time		Sensory	
Days Since Last		Mindset	
Other substances or factors		Sleep	
		Other	

DAILY RECAP / REFLECTION

DRAW OR WRITE

Date	

DOSE INFORMATION

Dose Day		Day off	
Substance			
Dosage			
Time			
Days Since Last			
Other substances or factors			

FEELING / EFFECTS

Focus	
Mood	
Creativity	
Sensory	
Mindset	
Sleep	
Other	

DAILY RECAP / REFLECTION

DRAW OR WRITE

Date	

DOSE INFORMATION

Dose Day		Day off	
Substance			
Dosage			
Time			
Days Since Last			
Other substances or factors			

FEELING / EFFECTS

Focus	
Mood	
Creativity	
Sensory	
Mindset	
Sleep	
Other	

DAILY RECAP / REFLECTION

DRAW OR WRITE

Date	

DOSE INFORMATION		
Dose Day	Day off	
Substance		
Dosage		
Time		
Days Since Last		
Other substances or factors		

FEELING / EFFECTS	
Focus	
Mood	
Creativity	
Sensory	
Mindset	
Sleep	
Other	

DAILY RECAP / REFLECTION

DRAW OR WRITE

Date	

DOSE INFORMATION

Dose Day		Day off	
Substance			
Dosage			
Time			
Days Since Last			
Other substances or factors			

FEELING / EFFECTS

Focus	
Mood	
Creativity	
Sensory	
Mindset	
Sleep	
Other	

DAILY RECAP / REFLECTION

DRAW OR WRITE

Date	

DOSE INFORMATION			FEELING / EFFECTS	
Dose Day		Day off	Focus	
Substance			Mood	
Dosage			Creativity	
Time			Sensory	
Days Since Last			Mindset	
Other substances or factors			Sleep	
			Other	

DAILY RECAP / REFLECTION

DRAW OR WRITE

Date	

DOSE INFORMATION

Dose Day		Day off	
Substance			
Dosage			
Time			
Days Since Last			
Other substances or factors			

FEELING / EFFECTS

Focus	
Mood	
Creativity	
Sensory	
Mindset	
Sleep	
Other	

DAILY RECAP / REFLECTION

DRAW OR WRITE

Date	

DOSE INFORMATION	

Dose Day		Day off	
Substance			
Dosage			
Time			
Days Since Last			
Other substances or factors			

FEELING / EFFECTS	
Focus	
Mood	
Creativity	
Sensory	
Mindset	
Sleep	
Other	

DAILY RECAP / REFLECTION

DRAW OR WRITE

Date	

DOSE INFORMATION

Dose Day		Day off	
Substance			
Dosage			
Time			
Days Since Last			
Other substances or factors			

FEELING / EFFECTS

Focus	
Mood	
Creativity	
Sensory	
Mindset	
Sleep	
Other	

DAILY RECAP / REFLECTION

DRAW OR WRITE

Date	

DOSE INFORMATION				FEELING / EFFECTS	
Dose Day		Day off		Focus	
Substance				Mood	
Dosage				Creativity	
Time				Sensory	
Days Since Last				Mindset	
Other substances or factors				Sleep	
				Other	

DAILY RECAP / REFLECTION

DRAW OR WRITE

Date	

DOSE INFORMATION		FEELING / EFFECTS	

Dose Day		Day off		Focus	
Substance				Mood	
Dosage				Creativity	
Time				Sensory	
Days Since Last				Mindset	
Other substances or factors				Sleep	
				Other	

DAILY RECAP / REFLECTION

DRAW OR WRITE

Date	

DOSE INFORMATION		FEELING / EFFECTS	
Dose Day	Day off	Focus	
Substance		Mood	
Dosage		Creativity	
Time		Sensory	
Days Since Last		Mindset	
Other substances or factors		Sleep	
		Other	

DAILY RECAP / REFLECTION

DRAW OR WRITE

Date	

DOSE INFORMATION			FEELING / EFFECTS	
Dose Day	Day off		Focus	
Substance			Mood	
Dosage			Creativity	
Time			Sensory	
Days Since Last			Mindset	
Other substances or factors			Sleep	
			Other	

DAILY RECAP / REFLECTION

DRAW OR WRITE

Date	

DOSE INFORMATION		FEELING / EFFECTS	
Dose Day	Day off	Focus	
Substance		Mood	
Dosage		Creativity	
Time		Sensory	
Days Since Last		Mindset	
Other substances or factors		Sleep	
		Other	

DAILY RECAP / REFLECTION

DRAW OR WRITE

Date	

DOSE INFORMATION

Dose Day		Day off	
Substance			
Dosage			
Time			
Days Since Last			
Other substances or factors			

FEELING / EFFECTS

Focus	
Mood	
Creativity	
Sensory	
Mindset	
Sleep	
Other	

DAILY RECAP / REFLECTION

DRAW OR WRITE

Date	

DOSE INFORMATION

Dose Day		Day off	
Substance			
Dosage			
Time			
Days Since Last			
Other substances or factors			

FEELING / EFFECTS

Focus	
Mood	
Creativity	
Sensory	
Mindset	
Sleep	
Other	

DAILY RECAP / REFLECTION

DRAW OR WRITE

Date	

DOSE INFORMATION

Dose Day		Day off	
Substance			
Dosage			
Time			
Days Since Last			
Other substances or factors			

FEELING / EFFECTS

Focus	
Mood	
Creativity	
Sensory	
Mindset	
Sleep	
Other	

DAILY RECAP / REFLECTION

DRAW OR WRITE

Date	

DOSE INFORMATION

Dose Day		Day off	
Substance			
Dosage			
Time			
Days Since Last			
Other substances or factors			

FEELING / EFFECTS

Focus	
Mood	
Creativity	
Sensory	
Mindset	
Sleep	
Other	

DAILY RECAP / REFLECTION

DRAW OR WRITE

Date	

DOSE INFORMATION			FEELING / EFFECTS	

Dose Day		Day off		Focus	
Substance				Mood	
Dosage				Creativity	
Time				Sensory	
Days Since Last				Mindset	
Other substances or factors				Sleep	
				Other	

DAILY RECAP / REFLECTION

DRAW OR WRITE

Date	

DOSE INFORMATION			FEELING / EFFECTS	
Dose Day		Day off	Focus	
Substance			Mood	
Dosage			Creativity	
Time			Sensory	
Days Since Last			Mindset	
Other substances or factors			Sleep	
			Other	

DAILY RECAP / REFLECTION

DRAW OR WRITE

Date	

DOSE INFORMATION

Dose Day		Day off	
Substance			
Dosage			
Time			
Days Since Last			
Other substances or factors			

FEELING / EFFECTS

Focus	
Mood	
Creativity	
Sensory	
Mindset	
Sleep	
Other	

DAILY RECAP / REFLECTION

DRAW OR WRITE

Date	

DOSE INFORMATION

Dose Day		Day off	
Substance			
Dosage			
Time			
Days Since Last			
Other substances or factors			

FEELING / EFFECTS

Focus	
Mood	
Creativity	
Sensory	
Mindset	
Sleep	
Other	

DAILY RECAP / REFLECTION

DRAW OR WRITE

Date	

DOSE INFORMATION

Dose Day		Day off	
Substance			
Dosage			
Time			
Days Since Last			
Other substances or factors			

FEELING / EFFECTS

Focus	
Mood	
Creativity	
Sensory	
Mindset	
Sleep	
Other	

DAILY RECAP / REFLECTION

DRAW OR WRITE

Date	

DOSE INFORMATION		

Dose Day		Day off	
Substance			
Dosage			
Time			
Days Since Last			
Other substances or factors			

FEELING / EFFECTS	
Focus	
Mood	
Creativity	
Sensory	
Mindset	
Sleep	
Other	

DAILY RECAP / REFLECTION

DRAW OR WRITE

Date	

DOSE INFORMATION			FEELING / EFFECTS	

Dose Day		Day off		Focus	
Substance				Mood	
Dosage				Creativity	
Time				Sensory	
Days Since Last				Mindset	
Other substances or factors				Sleep	
				Other	

DAILY RECAP / REFLECTION

DRAW OR WRITE

Date	

DOSE INFORMATION

Dose Day		Day off		
Substance				
Dosage				
Time				
Days Since Last				
Other substances or factors				

FEELING / EFFECTS

Focus	
Mood	
Creativity	
Sensory	
Mindset	
Sleep	
Other	

DAILY RECAP / REFLECTION

DRAW OR WRITE

Date	

DOSE INFORMATION

Dose Day		Day off	
Substance			
Dosage			
Time			
Days Since Last			
Other substances or factors			

FEELING / EFFECTS

Focus	
Mood	
Creativity	
Sensory	
Mindset	
Sleep	
Other	

DAILY RECAP / REFLECTION

DRAW OR WRITE

Date	

DOSE INFORMATION			FEELING / EFFECTS	
Dose Day	Day off		Focus	
Substance			Mood	
Dosage			Creativity	
Time			Sensory	
Days Since Last			Mindset	
Other substances or factors			Sleep	
			Other	

DAILY RECAP / REFLECTION

DRAW OR WRITE

Date	

DOSE INFORMATION

Dose Day		Day off	
Substance			
Dosage			
Time			
Days Since Last			
Other substances or factors			

FEELING / EFFECTS

Focus	
Mood	
Creativity	
Sensory	
Mindset	
Sleep	
Other	

DAILY RECAP / REFLECTION

DRAW OR WRITE

Date	

DOSE INFORMATION

Dose Day		Day off	
Substance			
Dosage			
Time			
Days Since Last			
Other substances or factors			

FEELING / EFFECTS

Focus	
Mood	
Creativity	
Sensory	
Mindset	
Sleep	
Other	

DAILY RECAP / REFLECTION

DRAW OR WRITE

Date	

DOSE INFORMATION

Dose Day		Day off	
Substance			
Dosage			
Time			
Days Since Last			
Other substances or factors			

FEELING / EFFECTS

Focus	
Mood	
Creativity	
Sensory	
Mindset	
Sleep	
Other	

DAILY RECAP / REFLECTION

DRAW OR WRITE

Date	

DOSE INFORMATION

Dose Day		Day off	
Substance			
Dosage			
Time			
Days Since Last			
Other substances or factors			

FEELING / EFFECTS

Focus	
Mood	
Creativity	
Sensory	
Mindset	
Sleep	
Other	

DAILY RECAP / REFLECTION

DRAW OR WRITE

Date	

DOSE INFORMATION			FEELING / EFFECTS	
Dose Day		Day off	Focus	
Substance			Mood	
Dosage			Creativity	
Time			Sensory	
Days Since Last			Mindset	
Other substances or factors			Sleep	
			Other	

DAILY RECAP / REFLECTION

DRAW OR WRITE

Date	

DOSE INFORMATION

Dose Day		Day off	
Substance			
Dosage			
Time			
Days Since Last			
Other substances or factors			

FEELING / EFFECTS

Focus	
Mood	
Creativity	
Sensory	
Mindset	
Sleep	
Other	

DAILY RECAP / REFLECTION

DRAW OR WRITE

Date	

DOSE INFORMATION

Dose Day		Day off	
Substance			
Dosage			
Time			
Days Since Last			
Other substances or factors			

FEELING / EFFECTS

Focus	
Mood	
Creativity	
Sensory	
Mindset	
Sleep	
Other	

DAILY RECAP / REFLECTION

DRAW OR WRITE

Date	

DOSE INFORMATION

Dose Day		Day off	
Substance			
Dosage			
Time			
Days Since Last			
Other substances or factors			

FEELING / EFFECTS

Focus	
Mood	
Creativity	
Sensory	
Mindset	
Sleep	
Other	

DAILY RECAP / REFLECTION

DRAW OR WRITE

	Date	

DOSE INFORMATION			FEELING / EFFECTS	
Dose Day	Day off		Focus	
Substance			Mood	
Dosage			Creativity	
Time			Sensory	
Days Since Last			Mindset	
Other substances or factors			Sleep	
			Other	

DAILY RECAP / REFLECTION

DRAW OR WRITE

Date	

DOSE INFORMATION			FEELING / EFFECTS		
Dose Day		Day off	Focus		
Substance			Mood		
Dosage			Creativity		
Time			Sensory		
Days Since Last			Mindset		
Other substances or factors			Sleep		
			Other		

DAILY RECAP / REFLECTION

DRAW OR WRITE

Date	

DOSE INFORMATION

Dose Day		Day off	
Substance			
Dosage			
Time			
Days Since Last			
Other substances or factors			

FEELING / EFFECTS

Focus	
Mood	
Creativity	
Sensory	
Mindset	
Sleep	
Other	

DAILY RECAP / REFLECTION

DRAW OR WRITE

Date	

DOSE INFORMATION				FEELING / EFFECTS	
Dose Day		Day off		Focus	
Substance				Mood	
Dosage				Creativity	
Time				Sensory	
Days Since Last				Mindset	
Other substances or factors				Sleep	
				Other	

DAILY RECAP / REFLECTION

DRAW OR WRITE

Date	

DOSE INFORMATION

Dose Day		Day off	
Substance			
Dosage			
Time			
Days Since Last			
Other substances or factors			

FEELING / EFFECTS

Focus	
Mood	
Creativity	
Sensory	
Mindset	
Sleep	
Other	

DAILY RECAP / REFLECTION

DRAW OR WRITE

Date	

DOSE INFORMATION			FEELING / EFFECTS	
Dose Day	Day off		Focus	
Substance			Mood	
Dosage			Creativity	
Time			Sensory	
Days Since Last			Mindset	
Other substances or factors			Sleep	
			Other	

DAILY RECAP / REFLECTION

DRAW OR WRITE

Date	

DOSE INFORMATION

Dose Day		Day off	
Substance			
Dosage			
Time			
Days Since Last			
Other substances or factors			

FEELING / EFFECTS

Focus	
Mood	
Creativity	
Sensory	
Mindset	
Sleep	
Other	

DAILY RECAP / REFLECTION

DRAW OR WRITE

Date	

DOSE INFORMATION

Dose Day		Day off	
Substance			
Dosage			
Time			
Days Since Last			
Other substances or factors			

FEELING / EFFECTS

Focus	
Mood	
Creativity	
Sensory	
Mindset	
Sleep	
Other	

DAILY RECAP / REFLECTION

DRAW OR WRITE

Date	

DOSE INFORMATION

Dose Day		Day off	
Substance			
Dosage			
Time			
Days Since Last			
Other substances or factors			

FEELING / EFFECTS

Focus	
Mood	
Creativity	
Sensory	
Mindset	
Sleep	
Other	

DAILY RECAP / REFLECTION

DRAW OR WRITE

Date	

DOSE INFORMATION

Dose Day		Day off	
Substance			
Dosage			
Time			
Days Since Last			
Other substances or factors			

FEELING / EFFECTS

Focus	
Mood	
Creativity	
Sensory	
Mindset	
Sleep	
Other	

DAILY RECAP / REFLECTION

DRAW OR WRITE

	Date	

DOSE INFORMATION			FEELING / EFFECTS	
Dose Day		Day off	Focus	
Substance			Mood	
Dosage			Creativity	
Time			Sensory	
Days Since Last			Mindset	
Other substances or factors			Sleep	
			Other	

DAILY RECAP / REFLECTION

DRAW OR WRITE

Date	

DOSE INFORMATION

Dose Day		Day off	
Substance			
Dosage			
Time			
Days Since Last			
Other substances or factors			

FEELING / EFFECTS

Focus	
Mood	
Creativity	
Sensory	
Mindset	
Sleep	
Other	

DAILY RECAP / REFLECTION

DRAW OR WRITE

Date	

DOSE INFORMATION

Dose Day		Day off	
Substance			
Dosage			
Time			
Days Since Last			
Other substances or factors			

FEELING / EFFECTS

Focus	
Mood	
Creativity	
Sensory	
Mindset	
Sleep	
Other	

DAILY RECAP / REFLECTION

DRAW OR WRITE

Date	

DOSE INFORMATION

Dose Day		Day off	
Substance			
Dosage			
Time			
Days Since Last			
Other substances or factors			

FEELING / EFFECTS

Focus	
Mood	
Creativity	
Sensory	
Mindset	
Sleep	
Other	

DAILY RECAP / REFLECTION

DRAW OR WRITE

Date	

DOSE INFORMATION		FEELING / EFFECTS	

Dose Day	Day off	Focus	
Substance		Mood	
Dosage		Creativity	
Time		Sensory	
Days Since Last		Mindset	
Other substances or factors		Sleep	
		Other	

DAILY RECAP / REFLECTION

DRAW OR WRITE

Date	

DOSE INFORMATION

Dose Day		Day off	
Substance			
Dosage			
Time			
Days Since Last			
Other substances or factors			

FEELING / EFFECTS

Focus	
Mood	
Creativity	
Sensory	
Mindset	
Sleep	
Other	

DAILY RECAP / REFLECTION

DRAW OR WRITE

Date	

DOSE INFORMATION

Dose Day		Day off	
Substance			
Dosage			
Time			
Days Since Last			
Other substances or factors			

FEELING / EFFECTS

Focus	
Mood	
Creativity	
Sensory	
Mindset	
Sleep	
Other	

DAILY RECAP / REFLECTION

DRAW OR WRITE

Date	

DOSE INFORMATION

Dose Day		Day off	
Substance			
Dosage			
Time			
Days Since Last			
Other substances or factors			

FEELING / EFFECTS

Focus	
Mood	
Creativity	
Sensory	
Mindset	
Sleep	
Other	

DAILY RECAP / REFLECTION

DRAW OR WRITE

Date	

DOSE INFORMATION

Dose Day		Day off	
Substance			
Dosage			
Time			
Days Since Last			
Other substances or factors			

FEELING / EFFECTS

Focus	
Mood	
Creativity	
Sensory	
Mindset	
Sleep	
Other	

DAILY RECAP / REFLECTION

DRAW OR WRITE

Date	

DOSE INFORMATION			FEELING / EFFECTS	
Dose Day	Day off		Focus	
Substance			Mood	
Dosage			Creativity	
Time			Sensory	
Days Since Last			Mindset	
Other substances or factors			Sleep	
			Other	

DAILY RECAP / REFLECTION

DRAW OR WRITE

Date	

DOSE INFORMATION

Dose Day		Day off	
Substance			
Dosage			
Time			
Days Since Last			
Other substances or factors			

FEELING / EFFECTS

Focus	
Mood	
Creativity	
Sensory	
Mindset	
Sleep	
Other	

DAILY RECAP / REFLECTION

DRAW OR WRITE

Date	

DOSE INFORMATION		

Dose Day		Day off	
Substance			
Dosage			
Time			
Days Since Last			
Other substances or factors			

FEELING / EFFECTS

Focus	
Mood	
Creativity	
Sensory	
Mindset	
Sleep	
Other	

DAILY RECAP / REFLECTION

DRAW OR WRITE

Date	

DOSE INFORMATION

Dose Day		Day off	
Substance			
Dosage			
Time			
Days Since Last			
Other substances or factors			

FEELING / EFFECTS

Focus	
Mood	
Creativity	
Sensory	
Mindset	
Sleep	
Other	

DAILY RECAP / REFLECTION

DRAW OR WRITE

Date	

DOSE INFORMATION

Dose Day		Day off	
Substance			
Dosage			
Time			
Days Since Last			
Other substances or factors			

FEELING / EFFECTS

Focus	
Mood	
Creativity	
Sensory	
Mindset	
Sleep	
Other	

DAILY RECAP / REFLECTION

DRAW OR WRITE

Date	

DOSE INFORMATION

Dose Day		Day off	
Substance			
Dosage			
Time			
Days Since Last			
Other substances or factors			

FEELING / EFFECTS

Focus	
Mood	
Creativity	
Sensory	
Mindset	
Sleep	
Other	

DAILY RECAP / REFLECTION

DRAW OR WRITE

Date	

DOSE INFORMATION

Dose Day		Day off	
Substance			
Dosage			
Time			
Days Since Last			
Other substances or factors			

FEELING / EFFECTS

Focus	
Mood	
Creativity	
Sensory	
Mindset	
Sleep	
Other	

DAILY RECAP / REFLECTION

DRAW OR WRITE

	Date	

DOSE INFORMATION		FEELING / EFFECTS	
Dose Day	Day off	Focus	
Substance		Mood	
Dosage		Creativity	
Time		Sensory	
Days Since Last		Mindset	
Other substances or factors		Sleep	
		Other	

DAILY RECAP / REFLECTION

DRAW OR WRITE

Date	

DOSE INFORMATION

Dose Day		Day off	
Substance			
Dosage			
Time			
Days Since Last			
Other substances or factors			

FEELING / EFFECTS

Focus	
Mood	
Creativity	
Sensory	
Mindset	
Sleep	
Other	

DAILY RECAP / REFLECTION

DRAW OR WRITE

NOTES

NOTE	
Date	**Nature / title of note**

NOTE	
Date	**Nature / title of note**

NOTE	
Date	**Nature / title of note**

NOTE	
Date	**Nature / title of note**

NOTE	
Date	**Nature / title of note**

NOTES

NOTE			
Date		Nature / title of note	

NOTE			
Date		Nature / title of note	

NOTE			
Date		Nature / title of note	

NOTE			
Date		Nature / title of note	

NOTE			
Date		Nature / title of note	

NOTES

NOTE		
Date		**Nature / title of note**

NOTE		
Date		**Nature / title of note**

NOTE		
Date		**Nature / title of note**

NOTE		
Date		**Nature / title of note**

NOTE		
Date		**Nature / title of note**

NOTES

NOTE		
Date		**Nature / title of note**

NOTE		
Date		**Nature / title of note**

NOTE		
Date		**Nature / title of note**

NOTE		
Date		**Nature / title of note**

NOTE		
Date		**Nature / title of note**

NOTES

NOTE		
Date		Nature / title of note

NOTE		
Date		Nature / title of note

NOTE		
Date		Nature / title of note

NOTE		
Date		Nature / title of note

NOTE		
Date		Nature / title of note

NOTES

NOTE		
Date		Nature / title of note

NOTE		
Date		Nature / title of note

NOTE		
Date		Nature / title of note

NOTE		
Date		Nature / title of note

NOTE		
Date		Nature / title of note

NOTES

NOTE	
Date	Nature / title of note

NOTE	
Date	Nature / title of note

NOTE	
Date	Nature / title of note

NOTE	
Date	Nature / title of note

NOTE	
Date	Nature / title of note

NOTES

NOTE		
Date		Nature / title of note

NOTE		
Date		Nature / title of note

NOTE		
Date		Nature / title of note

NOTE		
Date		Nature / title of note

NOTE		
Date		Nature / title of note

NOTES

NOTE	
Date	Nature / title of note

NOTE	
Date	Nature / title of note

NOTE	
Date	Nature / title of note

NOTE	
Date	Nature / title of note

NOTE	
Date	Nature / title of note

NOTES

NOTE		
Date		Nature / title of note

NOTE		
Date		Nature / title of note

NOTE		
Date		Nature / title of note

NOTE		
Date		Nature / title of note

NOTE		
Date		Nature / title of note

Made in United States
Troutdale, OR
09/01/2024